STARTING
ENDURANCE RIDING

by
Clare Wilde

Illustrations by
Carole Vincer

KENILWORTH PRESS

First published in Great Britain by
The Kenilworth Press Limited,
Addington, Buckingham, MK18 2JR

British Library Cataloguing in Publication Data
A catalogue record for this book is available from the British Library.

ISBN 1-872119-01-8

Typeset by Kenilworth Press

Printed in Great Britain by Westway Offset, Wembley

CONTENTS

Introduction

Endurance riding, in its modern form, began around 1955 when American rider Wendell Robie organised the first ever Tevis Cup 100-mile ride in the USA. The sport soon spread to the UK, and in the 1960s the first Golden Horseshoe ride was run over a distance of 50 miles.

Since those early days, the sport has flourished under the guidance of many individuals and different organisational bodies. The motto of the sport worldwide is 'to complete is to win', with the most important criteria for every rider being to finish with his or her horse fit to continue.

Today the sport consists of two basic types of ride, run over anything from 20 miles to 150 miles or more. The first of these is the non-competitive timed ride, which is ridden over a specified distance and within a set speed limit. Your horse has to pass certain veterinary requirements before, during and after the ride. These rides are called qualifiers, set speed or trail rides and provide a way for riders to gain experience before going on to race.

The second type of ride is a race ride. This is where all the riders set out together and race the whole distance, stopping to be checked by a vet at various designated points. The first rider home with a horse that passes the vet is the winner of the race.

At whatever level you choose to compete, the sport offers a unique opportunity for all to enjoy, because virtually anyone can take up endurance riding. Most people start out with the horse they already own and with no special qualifications, experience or equipment. The challenge is purely between you and your horse, the clock and the terrain. Endurance riding not only allows you to ride across some of the most beautiful countryside, but also offers all of us the opportunity to achieve goals of our own with no pressure to compete against others unless we choose to do so.

The most vital aspect of the sport is the emphasis it places upon education, through learning about the riding, preparation and management of your horse. There is no other sport that treats the welfare of the horse in quite the same way, and as a result endurance riding has pioneered some of the most modern advances in equine management techniques.

Whatever it is about endurance riding that attracts you, a sport that offers so much to all kinds of riders is certainly worth trying. Who knows – you may find yourself bitten by the endurance bug and go on to make the sport a way of life!

Starting out

At entry level, anyone can enjoy endurance riding. You don't need any special equipment or any particular kind of horse. As long as your horse's normal tack fits well and is in good repair, this is usually fine. However, it is worth checking the rules to find out what riders must wear - generally it is a regulation hard hat, jodhpurs of some kind, and either boots with a half-inch heel or stirrups that are caged, to allow for other types of footwear.

Any sound horse with a reasonable level of fitness should be able to complete a 20- or 25-mile ride without any difficulty. When you look at experienced endurance riders, you will see that they all ride in a wide variety of equipment and that many ride Arab or Arab-type horses. However, to begin with, it is important to work with what you have to find out whether you and your horse

enjoy the challenge of endurance riding.

As long as your horse is basically sound and has a fairly even temperament, he should be able to start endurance work. Heavier types of horse or pony will tend to retain heat and may therefore be less able to maintain a good speed over very long distances, but this should not be an issue for your first few rides.

If, however, your horse has some sort of physical problem such as navicular disease, joint problems or an injury which may cause him any difficulty, it is not really fair to place him under the extra strains that endurance riding will bring. At an organised ride, every horse has to pass the vet at least twice and must be sound, so it is worth checking with your own vet at home if you feel that your horse has a particular problem.

Assessing your horse

No horse is perfect. Even if you are lucky enough to have at home the right type of horse – one who has a relaxed attitude, economical, floating paces and loves his work – he is bound to have a lump or bump somewhere! Soundness and reasonable conformation are all that are required to start with, along with a temperament that will enable you both to enjoy the sport.

The best types of horse for endurance tend to have a long, economical and athletic stride that enables them to cover the ground without too much effort. They also tend to be fairly small (up to around 15.2hh) and wiry, with lean, flat muscles and deep chests. All of these physical attributes predispose the horse to being better able to cope with prolonged athletic work.

However, there are many horses in endurance who fall far to either side of this ideal. Cobs, ponies, Thoroughbreds and everything in between can be seen competing. It is fair to say, though, that horses with choppy strides, action peculiarities or naturally heavy frames and big muscles will find higher distances and speeds more challenging.

It is important to tailor your management and preparation according to your type of horse. For example, a heavy horse with a thick coat and a very short stride may need more preparation and careful management than a leaner, more athletic type, who will tend not to tire as quickly.

LEFT: Cob type with a round stride.
BELOW: Lighter-framed horse with a longer, more economical stride.

Feet and shoeing

As long as your horse's feet are in good condition and have been well cared for by your farrier, he should be able to manage his first rides without any special requirements.

The most important aspects of shoeing for endurance riding are protection and balance. Both sets of your horse's feet should be as close to a pair as possible, and have a good hoof/pastern axis. Many endurance horses compete in ordinary shoes, without any special alterations, right up to top level.

It is a good idea, however, to make sure that your farrier knows that you are going to do some endurance riding, so that he can make any adjustments he feels may be needed to protect your horse's feet.

Look at the way your horse's shoes fit to see that they provide plenty of support for his heels.

His hooves should also be in super condition. If he tends to have problems keeping his shoes on, due to weak or crumbly hoof horn, then attend to his diet by giving him the right supplements for good horn growth before expecting him to cope with the extra training for endurance riding.

Horses with thin soles or very flat feet may need to have pads fitted to enable them to work comfortably on stony terrain.

Horses who wear their shoes unevenly due to their action, may need tungsten-tipped nails in the corners of their shoes. This will help to prevent them wearing down so quickly. For longer distances, some endurance horses wear wide-webbed shoes, which provide a greater weight-bearing surface in contact with the ground and a little more protection for the hoof.

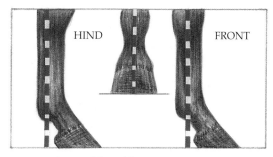

ABOVE: A good hoof/pastern axis is vital to help absorb concussion (approx. 50-55°).
BELOW: Good hoof horn (left) and crumbly, broken horn.

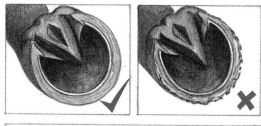

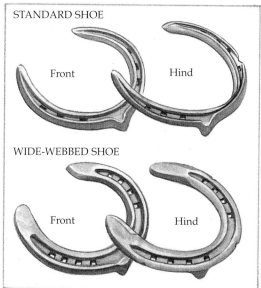

Standard shoes, which many endurance horses wear, and wide-webbed shoes, which offer a little more protection to the wall, sole and heel.

Basic health care

Your horse must be healthy in order to get fit. Pay attention to his worming, teeth and vaccinations before you begin. There are a number of checks on your horse's health which are useful in endurance riding. The first is his **pulse and heart rate**, which you should monitor throughout his training. An endurance horse's pulse rate is one of the criteria by which the vet judges his fitness, so get to know your horse's rate early on and check it daily.

As he gets fitter, the horse's pulse rate drops. If the rate is higher than usual, it may be a sign that something is wrong.

Pulse rate is also a useful gauge of fitness. If you take it directly on arrival home after riding and then again ten minutes later, by the second check it should be falling to its normal resting rate. It will fall back to its resting rate more quickly as the horse gains fitness, but may stay elevated for longer if he has been under more stress than usual, if the weather conditions have changed, or if he is becoming unwell.

Other metabolic parameters to monitor include **temperature** and respiration. I take my horse's temperature when I begin training to establish a base level, and then if he ever appears off colour I can make a comparison.

You can check **respiration rate** simply by watching your horse's ribcage move as he breathes. At rest, it should remain fairly constant, but he may pant on a hot day and breathe quickly when working.

Throughout training, keep a close eye on the condition of your horse's skin, particularly his heels, which may show signs of cracking or wear and tear during training. Horses with pink skin in their heels may suffer from cracked heels through exposure to the wet and mud.

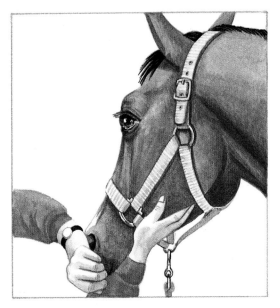

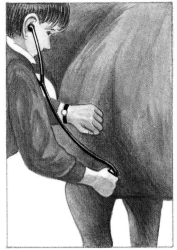

There are two ways to take a pulse: either with your fingers under the jaw, or with a stethoscope behind his elbow. A healthy horse has a resting pulse rate of 30-44 beats per minute. At first it may take you a little time to find his pulse using a stethoscope.

Check his mouth for possible bruising. A sore mouth may indicate that a change of bit is needed to make your horse more comfortable.

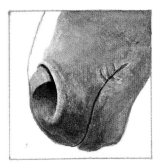

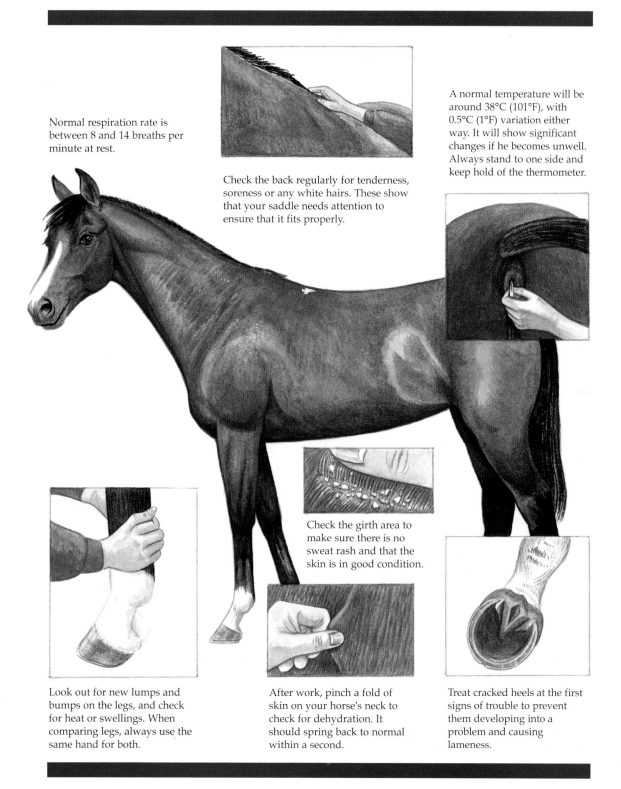

Normal respiration rate is between 8 and 14 breaths per minute at rest.

Check the back regularly for tenderness, soreness or any white hairs. These show that your saddle needs attention to ensure that it fits properly.

A normal temperature will be around 38°C (101°F), with 0.5°C (1°F) variation either way. It will show significant changes if he becomes unwell. Always stand to one side and keep hold of the thermometer.

Check the girth area to make sure there is no sweat rash and that the skin is in good condition.

Look out for new lumps and bumps on the legs, and check for heat or swellings. When comparing legs, always use the same hand for both.

After work, pinch a fold of skin on your horse's neck to check for dehydration. It should spring back to normal within a second.

Treat cracked heels at the first signs of trouble to prevent them developing into a problem and causing lameness.

Basic schooling and education

Your horse's basic schooling, if he is of a reasonable age, should be fairly well established. However, it is worth practising with the kind of hazards you may meet across open countryside.

Out on a ride you may have to cross bridges of all kinds, open and close gates, cross railway lines, or ride through water. Try to introduce your horse to all of these different sights and experiences during your training rides at home. This will help to make sure that you are both happy and confident about dealing with them out on the trail.

Gates are one of the most notorious hazards on endurance rides and it is a good idea to train your horse to help you to open and close them without you having to get off. On some rides this can result in an awful lot of extra work for you, and a lot of time wasted if your horse won't stand to let you open and close each gate that you meet.

Find out if your horse is happy to be passed from either direction by other horses, possibly in packs, and to work alone or in company. If necessary practise this at home.

OPENING AND CLOSING A GATE

Many horses are nervous about crossing water for the first time, but on a ride this offers a valuable opportunity to drink. Try to practise this at home if you know you may have to cross a river.

Handy schooling extras

There are a few techniques which can come in useful for endurance riding, such as teaching your horse to neck-rein, Western style. This can make life easier when out on the trail and save time when it comes to turning corners in a safe and balanced way.

Use a variety of other schooling exercises at home to train your horse to work in a supple, relaxed and rounded way in the school and to learn to move away from your leg laterally (sideways). This will build up his muscles correctly and help to ensure that he carries himself economically; it will also make him more useful and responsive when out in open country.

It is a good idea to set up a mock vetting or two at home so that your horse will be quite at ease on his first ride. Practise trotting him up, checking him for lumps and bumps, picking up his feet and taking his pulse. If possible, get a stranger to do this so that your horse won't be too surprised and will behave when he meets the vet at a ride.

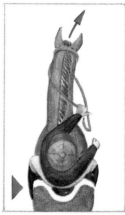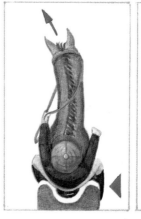

Neck-reining is handy out on the trail and can be quickly and simply taught at home in a paddock or school.

Teach your horse to trot out actively and sensibly for you at home, so that he will be easy to handle at a vetting.

It is also a good idea to practise cooling down your horse at home, pouring water from plastic 'slosh' bottles over his neck and shoulders to keep him cool.

Fitness and conditioning

Here is a basic fitness programme to prepare for a 20-mile ride. You can compare your own horse's fitness level with each stage below to see where you need to begin. A horse who is already fit and working at Week 10 level or above should be perfectly able to cope with his first rides.

Be sure to vary his routine as much as possible to keep him interested. Take

NOTES	MON	TUESDAY	WEDNESDAY
Week 1: All early walking work should be done actively, in a good outline and on fairly good going.		20 minutes flat walk	25 minutes flat walk
Week 2: Start to make use of gradients or gentle hills as his fitness improves.		5 minutes walk including some hills (same both days)	
Week 3: Once he has a basic level of fitness, begin to introduce some short periods of steady trotting on the flat.		50 minutes flat walk including some steady trot (same both days)	
Week 4: Now you can begin trotting up some gentle hills. Always increase time and distance worked before speed.		1 hour steady work including gentle hillwork	45 minutes gentle schooling
Week 5: If he is ready, you can add some steady canter on the flat.	DAY OFF	1 hour including up to 20 minutes trot, or steady lungeing	45 minutes including some trotting uphill
Week 6: Now begin to ask for the occasional short canter on your uphill stretches.		1 hour including gentle schooling work on balancing trot	45 minutes including some gentle canter uphill
Week 7: This is a good time to work on keeping up a steady trot or canter for longer stretches at a time.		1 hour 10 minutes schooling or flatwork lesson	50 minutes including more uphill canter
Week 8: Work on steadily increasing the distances you cover in training, to prepare for your first ride.		1 hour 20 minutes gentle hack	1 hour including steady schooling or jumping
Week 9: Stretches of uphill work in steady trot or canter should be increased a little to make his heart work harder.		1 hour 20 minutes including schooling or flatwork lesson	1 hour including steady uphill canter
Week 10: By now you can practise a training route of 15 miles to assess your horse's fitness for your first ride.		1 hour 30 minutes gentle hack	1 hour including some steady lungeing at canter

advantage of any hills, which will increase the effort he has to make – don't continually work on the flat. In training, take care always to walk down hills. Watch for signs of stress, and if in doubt, drop back a stage. You are aiming to take part in a ride of 20 miles at 6-7mph, which will take you around three hours to ride, so don't overdo the training and take a tired horse to compete.

THURSDAY	FRI	SATURDAY	SUNDAY
minutes : walk		30 minutes walk incorporating some gentle slopes or hills (same both days)	
minutes : walk		45 minutes walk including some hillwork (same both days)	
minutes luding some ...s and steady t		55 minutes – 1 hour including some hills and up to 10 minutes steady trot (same both days)	
minutes : walk	↑	1 hour 10 minutes including steady trot up to 7 miles at 6mph	1 hour steady exercise as Saturday, include some jumping
...our gentle ...hooling ...cluding some ...ady canter	DAY OFF	1 hour 10 minutes including up to 25 minutes trotting	As Saturday, but 1 hour 20 minutes, with some steady canter
...our 10 minutes ...cluding some ...t – up to ... minutes total		1 hour 20 minutes including up to 20 minutes steady lungeing or jumping	1 hour 30 minutes including steady uphill canter
...our 20 minutes ...ady lungeing ... jumping		Up to 10 miles at 7mph: 1 hour 30 minutes. Use hills, keeping up steady trot and canter (same both days)	
...our 20 minutes ...cluding some ...ster work in ...nter		1 hour 45 minutes including some steady canter	1 hour 30 minutes, as Saturday, plus hillwork in trot
...hour 30 ...inutes ...ntle ...ck	↓	2 hours including some lungeing at trot	1 hour 45 minutes including steady uphill trot and canter
...hour 30 minutes ...cluding some ...hooling		2 hours 15 minutes including steady canter and trotting. Up to 15 miles at 7mph	2 hours steady work including some hillwork at trot

Feeding

There are no special feeding requirements for a horse working at 20- or 25-mile level. As long as you are giving your horse a good, basic diet, which provides all the necessary nutrients for his body, there is no need to worry about adding anything extra to his diet. Always remember to increase the amount of feed given following an increase in his workload, and to make any changes to his diet gradually.

If you are bringing a completely unfit horse up for work, then he will have to be introduced slowly to hard feed as he works. He may well need to lose a little excess weight early on in his training programme, but should be allowed access to plenty of long fibre. Use your eye to gauge how much to feed, and adjust feed according to his workload and condition.

Your horse's feeding requirements are based upon as much long fibre, in the form of hay, haylage or grass, as he will eat. This is the staple element of any healthy diet and hard feed is added only to cater for the increased nutrient requirements that come with extra work.

His hard feed may consist of a good coarse mix, a complete cube or a mixture of straight feeds such as barley or oats. Any of these should ideally be fed with soaked sugar beet. Sugar beet forms the basis of almost every endurance horse's hard feed, for a number of reasons. It provides fibre and energy as well as a base to keep down any dust in feeds, and increases the palatability of each meal. It also aids the retention of water in the gut, helping to keep your horse adequately hydrated when training and competing.

In summer, it is a good idea to add salt or a training electrolyte to your horse's feed. This ensures that any minerals he loses through sweat are replaced, enabling his body to continue to function efficiently and preventing deficiencies. Although he is unlikely to sweat much at this stage, it is worth remembering to include electrolytes in his feed at home as well as offering them in water on a ride if he does tend to sweat. However, you should never offer electrolytes to a horse who is already very dehydrated.

Your horse may have a particular requirement for a vitamin or mineral supplement, perhaps to encourage healthy hoof growth. Feeding oil is a good way to provide energy and maintain condition without adding any extra weight of feed; you can use any kind of vegetable oil or cod liver oil.

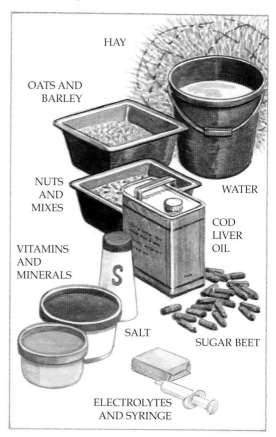

HAY

OATS AND BARLEY

NUTS AND MIXES

WATER

COD LIVER OIL

VITAMINS AND MINERALS

SALT

SUGAR BEET

ELECTROLYTES AND SYRINGE

The horse's equipment

No special equipment is needed to start endurance riding. As long as your tack fits and is in good condition, then this is all you need. It is wise to compete in what your horse normally wears at home and without too many extras. The less tack your horse wears, the less there is to potentially rub or cause a problem; also the less there is to clean and the more comfortable the horse will be.

Always check the ride rules to make sure that your tack meets the regulations.

If you begin competing frequently, then you may wish to consider buying some specialist tack. In endurance riding, the emphasis is placed on comfort, light weight and durability. There are a number of specialist saddles available, all designed to spread the rider's weight across more of the horse's back, making him more comfortable, as well as placing you in a better riding position.

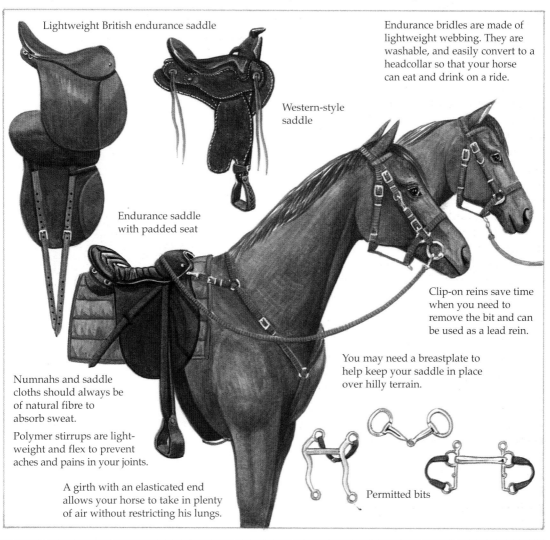

Lightweight British endurance saddle

Endurance bridles are made of lightweight webbing. They are washable, and easily convert to a headcollar so that your horse can eat and drink on a ride.

Western-style saddle

Endurance saddle with padded seat

Clip-on reins save time when you need to remove the bit and can be used as a lead rein.

Numnahs and saddle cloths should always be of natural fibre to absorb sweat.

Polymer stirrups are lightweight and flex to prevent aches and pains in your joints.

You may need a breastplate to help keep your saddle in place over hilly terrain.

A girth with an elasticated end allows your horse to take in plenty of air without restricting his lungs.

Permitted bits

The rider's equipment

For early rides, you simply need basic, safe riding clothes that are comfortable for you and conform to the ride rules. Standard endurance riding wear tends to be a regulation hard hat, a rugby or cross-country shirt, jodhpurs or riding tights, and boots. Your boots must have a half-inch heel, or you need to have caged-front stirrups, which will allow you to wear riding trainers safely.

It is a good idea to carry a bag around your waist in which to keep some first-aid kit, and a map case to carry over your shoulder for the route map.

There is a whole range of specialist clothing and footwear for endurance riders, all aimed at providing comfort and durability but using lightweight materials. The most popular choice of clothing is a pair of Lycra, padded riding tights, and a ventilated hat to help keep you cool on a long ride.

Footwear comes in a wide variety of styles and types but the most popular choice is a soft riding trainer and a pair of half-chaps. This combination allows you to get off your horse and run comfortably, if necessary, as well as offering flexibility and protection for your lower leg.

Riders like to look smart and stay comfortable, so clothing varies a little according to individual preference.

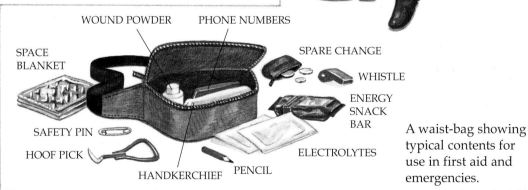

SPACE BLANKET

WOUND POWDER

PHONE NUMBERS

SPARE CHANGE

WHISTLE

ENERGY SNACK BAR

SAFETY PIN

HOOF PICK

HANDKERCHIEF

PENCIL

ELECTROLYTES

A waist-bag showing typical contents for use in first aid and emergencies.

Rider fitness and preparation

As well as preparing your horse to compete, you must prepare yourself. It's all about making life as easy as possible for your horse. If you have any doubts about your own riding ability, then take a few lessons before you ask your horse to carry you further and faster for longer. You also need to learn some basic map-reading skills to study the ride route.

It is important to maintain your own calm during a ride, so that you can listen to your horse and ride your own ride. Learn to concentrate on pacing your horse according to his abilities and fitness, rather than being carried along by those around you. Gauging your horse's speed is easy enough to learn at home by riding a measured distance, say half a mile, in different gaits and timing how long it takes you to cover the distance.

It is important that you take care of yourself on a ride and maintain your own physical and mental well-being by eating and drinking regularly, and not allowing yourself to become over-tired or dehydrated. There are a variety of tasty, nutritious performance foods available such as carbohydrate drinks and bars, which are ideal for endurance riders. These provide plenty of energy without too much sugar.

Practise your riding technique and learn to work in harmony with your horse, maintaining good balance. This makes life easier and helps him to cover the distance.

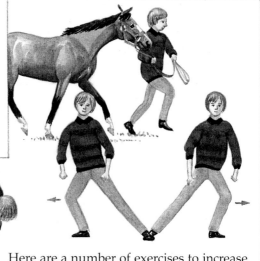

Here are a number of exercises to increase suppleness, gently stretching the tendons and muscles in your legs. Running with your horse whilst out training increases your overall fitness.

Back-up crew

On some rides it is compulsory to have a helper or back-up crew with you, but at every ride having some assistance makes life much easier for you and your horse. For short distances at slow speeds your needs will be fairly basic, but this is where your crew learns how to help take care of your horse. At this stage, you won't need to take too much equipment with you, but you can concentrate on learning about caring for your horse.

The main role for your crew will be to meet you every five miles or so, to make sure that you and the horse are well. Your helper should offer both of you a drink and something to eat, and slosh the horse down with bottles of water to help keep him cool and keep his pulse rate down. In reality, your horse is unlikely to drink or eat on a 20-mile ride, but if it's a very hot day, he may be thirsty. Your crew should also keep an eye on the horse for any cuts or other small injuries which may need attention.

It is a good idea to practise a crewing pit-stop at home so that your crew can get used to offering your horse drinks, washing and sponging him down, and

perhaps checking his feet if you have ridden over a particularly stony stretch. This way, you will feel confident at a ride that your horse is used to the routine, that the routine works for you, and that your crew is used to the horse!

It is important that your crew can map-read in order to navigate from one meeting place to another, as well as being able to handle your horse confidently and calmly. It also helps if your crew is knowledgeable enough to recognise signs of fatigue in both you and your horse.

It is a good idea for your crew to carry a few essential spares, such as stirrup leathers or reins, a rug and a first-aid kit for horse and rider. They should also have containers of drinking water for the horse, buckets, bottles for sloshing and cooling down, sponges for washing down, and emergency items like a protective hoof boot in case you lose a shoe out on the trail.

TYPICAL BACK-UP CREW EQUIPMENT

Choosing and entering a ride

You should aim to take part in a first ride over a distance of either 20 or 25 miles. Choose a ride that is within easy travelling distance of your home. The terrain should be similar to the type you are used to training over: a flat-trained horse may not cope well with a steep, hilly area. Study the calendar and pick a ride whose date coincides with your horse's fitness. Enter in good time to make sure you secure a place on the ride. The week before, have your horse freshly shod and check that your equipment is in good condition. Pack your kit the day before, so that all you need to do on the day is load up and go.

Your details will be sent to you, including your number, vetting and start times, and route map.

Work out a table of times for reaching each checkpoint or pit-stop at minimum speed.

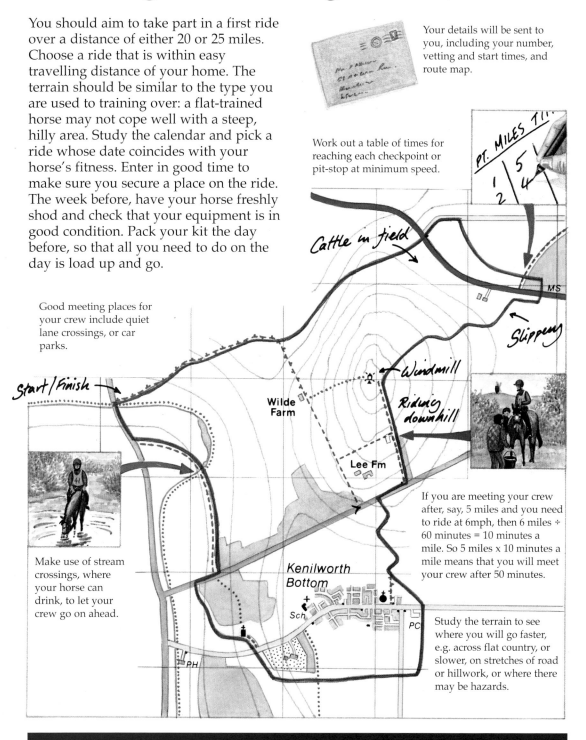

Good meeting places for your crew include quiet lane crossings, or car parks.

Make use of stream crossings, where your horse can drink, to let your crew go on ahead.

If you are meeting your crew after, say, 5 miles and you need to ride at 6mph, then 6 miles ÷ 60 minutes = 10 minutes a mile. So 5 miles x 10 minutes a mile means that you will meet your crew after 50 minutes.

Study the terrain to see where you will go faster, e.g. across flat country, or slower, on stretches of road or hillwork, or where there may be hazards.

19

Ride day

On the day of your first ride, leave home in plenty of time so that you reach the venue at least half an hour before your vetting. When you arrive and before you unload your horse, go and collect your number from the secretary and check out the venue, so that you know where to find the vet, farrier and tack inspector, and the start of the ride.

Once you unload your horse, walk him round gently and let him have a good look at everything, so he gets used to the sights and smells of the venue, before you take him to the vet.

The vet will take your horse's pulse rate, pinch his skin to test for dehydration, and check him all over for lumps and bumps, including his legs, back and girth areas. He may look in his mouth to check for bruising, and may pick up his feet to examine his shoes before trotting him up for soundness. Make sure that you trot your horse up steadily and on a long rein so that the vet can see his usual action. Try not to get between your horse and the vet, as you will prevent the vet from getting a good look at the way your horse moves.

You may also be required to visit the ride farrier, whose job is to check your horse's shoes before you are allowed to set off. In addition a tack inspector may be appointed to check that your kit is safe and meets the ride rules.

Once through the necessary checks, then it's time to tack up and warm up your horse gently. Go to the start a little early so that you are ready to set off at the right time. It is a good idea to set your watch to 12 o'clock as you start, so you can see your elapsed riding time at a glance.

Let your horse have a good look round so that he will be relaxed at the vetting.

The vet will follow a set procedure of checks to make sure your horse is fit to start the ride.

REMEMBER:
- Trot him on a loose rein.
- Stay as straight as possible.
- Stay by his side, not in front.
- Make sure the vet can see his normal action.
- Keep the pace steady and even.

Your own ride

Once you're out on the trail, take the first couple of miles steadily to allow your horse's muscles to warm up thoroughly. The aim is to get round with as much fun and as little hassle as possible, and to have enough faith in your preparation to be relaxed and enjoy your ride.

Pace your horse as consistently as possible, and ride your own ride exactly as you would over this distance at home, without getting towed along by faster horses. Your aim is to stay at a steady speed to help your horse conserve his energy. Some novices tend to rush out and then walk back in their panic to cover the distance, but this will not help your horse or teach either of you about pacing and economy of energy.

Ride carefully, listening to your horse all the time, and take advantage of your pit-stops with your crew to drink, eat and make sure that your horse is cool, which will help to keep his pulse rate down. Remember to be polite to other riders on the trail – there are plenty of friends to be made in endurance riding.

After the ride, wash your horse off and make him as clean and comfortable as possible. How you do this will depend upon the weather - if it is cold, he will need rugging up and walking gently to prevent him from stiffening up. If it is hot, he will need lots of washing off, and to stand in the shade to help him cool down. The priorities are to return his pulse rate to normal, and to make him comfortable, relaxed and happy.

Take your horse to the vet for his post-ride presentation at your allotted time and, once your day is over, remember to thank all the officials and organisers who made it possible for you to have such a wonderful ride. And don't forget to return your number and collect your rosette!

Set out steadily and remember to pace your horse as you would at home.

After the ride, make your horse as comfortable as possible by getting him clean and dry, ready for the vet. Massaging his muscles and walking him gently will help to keep him from getting stiff.

Post-ride care

When you arrive home following your ride, it is important that your horse is allowed to stretch his legs and unwind before being stabled for the night. Many riders neglect to do this and put their horse straight back in his stable. It is helpful for his muscles, and his mind, to have a little quiet relaxation with a gentle stretch in his field before he is stabled for the night. Tired muscles will have the opportunity to ease off a little with some gentle walking. This also helps to get the muscles of his gut moving again by allowing him to graze, as well as to roll and relax!

It is essential to make sure that your horse has plenty of rest and relaxation during the competition season. If a horse is not allowed adequate recovery time the physical wear and tear of endurance work can have a cumulative effect.

Massaging your horse's legs will increase circulation and help to eliminate puffiness. If checking for heat, however, use the same hand to compare both legs.

His feed should be reduced on the days that he rests. Generally I would recommend a day's rest for each ten miles he has covered, but following his first ride he may need three days off. During these few days, make sure that he is sound, has recovered his energy and is in good physical condition before you commence work again.

Go over your horse thoroughly. Check his mouth, his back, his girth area and his heels thoroughly and make sure that he has no new lumps or bumps on his legs. If he does have any injuries, then it is sensible to allow them to heal before you start work again, as this may worsen such conditions.

On his first day back in work it is a good idea is to start with some gentle or easy exercise, such as a 45-minute hack. This will let you know how well he has recovered and how fit he is feeling before you pick up his training programme where you left off.

Remember to take care of all your equipment; use your horse's rest days to clean and check all your tack and crewing gear. Make sure that everything is clean, dry and comfortable for him when he starts work again.

Prevention and treatment of injury

If, for any reason, your horse is spun by the vet on your first ride, it is a good idea to take stock of the reasons why and to remedy the situation so that your next attempt is successful.

If your horse was simply very tired and had a high pulse rate, it is likely that either he was not fit enough to cover the distance, or that the terrain was tougher than it is at home. It may also have been exceptionally hot. The only way to avoid a repetition is to get your horse fitter and used to the right type of terrain before attempting the same distance again.

A high heart rate may also be as a result of excitement. This is more a question of experience, careful handling and taking your horse to more rides. Gradually he will get used to what goes on and won't get so excited in future.

Minor lameness is often the result of either stone bruising or an over-tired or pulled muscle. As long as the ride vet has told you what the problem is, then follow his advice and give your horse plenty of rest before easing him back into work gently. If the injury is more serious, then your own vet should be called in when you get home.

If the skin does not return to normal after a pinch test this indicates a bad case of dehydration; even a slow return to normal can indicate some water loss.

Cold treatments such as clay and ice can refresh and restore over-exerted legs in the couple of days after a ride.

 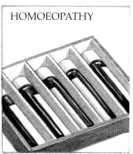  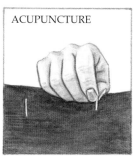

| HERBS | HOMOEOPATHY | MAGNET THERAPY | ACUPUNCTURE |

Many non-specific problems, such as pain from bruising or aching muscles, can be treated with homoeopathic remedies such as arnica tablets and lotion. Some endurance riders use complementary therapies as a matter of course, to deal with minor injuries, combat symptoms of fatigue and to help bring a horse back to condition.

What next?

Most people enjoy their early experiences so much that they are well and truly bitten by the endurance riding bug following their first ride. They want to go on to ride further, faster, farther afield. How soon you enter your next ride should be dictated by your own horse's recovery, but I would recommend riding the same distance on several occasions, allowing a few weeks between each ride, before you go on to try a higher distance.

It is important to make sure that your horse is coping easily with each progressive increase in mileage before you go on to the next one, or compete over more difficult terrain. Pushing any horse to do too much, too soon will simply result in injury or breakdown.

If your horse is really not suited to endurance riding, he may begin to struggle with the longer distances. It is up to you to decide whether you enjoy yourself by sticking to shorter rides, or if you want to go on to tackle much longer distances. When you reach this point you may have to decide to buy a purpose-bred horse, and begin to invest in some specialist equipment.

Over about 40 miles, the demands placed upon both you and your horse will begin to increase, and this is when your whole regime needs to be tailored towards real performance management, both in terms of your horse's training, management, diet and nutrition, and in your own fitness and equipment.

Race riding, in which you will be competing at higher speeds, demands a higher level of preparation and attention to detail. There are a few marathon races over 26 miles, but the majority of races are run from 40 or 50 miles, up to 100 miles in one day. There are no short-cuts. Training a horse to the kind of fitness required to compete over 100 miles takes several years.

Most riders will set their own personal goals, be it taking part in a specific ride, riding a certain distance, or clocking up a given number of miles in a year. Whatever your aim, it is important to remember at all times that the welfare of your horse is paramount. Endurance riding is all about having a wonderful time with your horse out in the countryside, and achieving goals through fulfilling your own personal challenges, as opposed to winning big prizes.

Good luck, and have fun!